¿QUÉ PASÓ?

¿QUÉ PASÓ?

An English-Spanish Guide for Medical Personnel

Martin P. Kantrowitz, M.D.

Antonio Mondragón

William Lord Coleman, M.D.

Fourth edition, revised and expanded

University of New Mexico Press / Albuquerque

Library of Congress Cataloging in Publication Data

Kantrowitz, Martin P., 1942–
  Qué pasó?

  1. Spanish language–Conversation and phrase books
(for medical personnel).
I. Mondragón, Antonio, 1938–   .
II. Coleman, William Lord, 1943–   .
III. Title.
[DNLM: 1. Medicine–Phrases–Spanish. W 13 k16q]
PC4120.M3K3   1983   468.3'421'02461   83-14670

ISBN 0-8263-0725-6

Photographs, William Lord Coleman

Tenth paperbound printing, 2001

Contents

Preface

The essential ingredient in good medical care is good communication between patients and medical personnel. We wrote *¿Qué Pasó?* in order to facilitate this communication. The book developed as a result of examining the experience of the Spanish-speaking patient who comes into the emergency room unable to speak or understand English. Such an experience is both confusing and frightening for the patient. The situation is equally frustrating to hospital personnel attempting to communicate with this patient or his/her family.

¿Qué Pasó? is designed for use in the clinic, the emergency room, the physician's office, and at the patient's bedside. It will be valuable to individuals with little or no Spanish-language background as well as to those who have a more thorough understanding of the language. This edition features the proper way to ask questions and includes probable answers. Many questions are phrased so that a "yes" or "no," a number, or a date will provide the appropriate answer. We have included essential phrases as well as questions and answers to enable the medical person to work up twenty-three of the most commonly presented complaints. The information is offered in an easy-to-use format with special emphasis on keeping the questions and phrases as concise and easy to pronounce as possible. Room is provided between all lines so that the user may write in local expressions. Southwestern localisms are included in brackets. The convenient size, the conciseness, and the light weight of *¿Qué Pasó?* allow it to be carried about easily in the pocket or instrument bag and used readily in the clinical situation. Moreover, the cover material is washable.

Since the publication of the first edition of *¿Qué Pasó?* the nature and composition of the Spanish-speaking population in the United States has changed. The text has been revised accordingly, to make this book as useful to physicians in the 1980s as it was in the 1970s. The third edition was expanded to include a larger vocabulary as well as workups on family planning, overdose/poisoning, and the unconscious patient. The fourth edition includes new pediatric workups to help health-care providers better care for their pediatric patients.

¿Qué Pasó? can be used with almost all Spanish-speaking people. It would be best to take a few minutes to ask a Spanish-speaking acquaintance the correct way to pronounce Spanish vowels and consonants in your locale. Once you have done this, you will find that Spanish words sound exactly as they are written.

It is important to remember that the Spanish language is basically a polite one. Thus, in Spanish, form is as important as content in establishing effective rapport with the patient. We have attempted to convey this politeness in the translations offered in *¿Qué Pasó?* Therefore the translations are not always a literal counterpart of the accompanying English; rather the emphasis has been on communicating the same meaning in Spanish as that implied by the English phrase or question.

We would appreciate any comments that the users of *¿Qué Pasó?* have about this edition, and we welcome suggestions for use in future editions.

¿Qué Pasó? will be indispensable to all medical care delivery personnel and students in health-related fields. It will also be helpful to the traveler to any Spanish-speaking land.

We would like to thank Beth Gard, our first editor at the University of New Mexico Press, and Patricio Vives, M.D., The Children's Hospital and South End Health Center, Boston, Mass., for their assistance.

Martin P. Kantrowitz, M.D.
Antonio Mondragón
William Lord Coleman, M.D.

Good Health for Everyone!
¡Buena Salud a Todos!

1

Common Phrases

These are very basic phrases intended for greeting the patient and directing him or her to the waiting room, examining room, or office.

For those with little Spanish:

I speak very little Spanish. Please speak slowly and, when possible, answer with "yes" or "no."	*Yo hablo muy poco español. Por favor, hable despacio y, si puede, conteste con "sí" o "no."*
Good morning	*Buenos días*
Good afternoon	*Buenas tardes (before dark)*
Good night (greeting)	*Buenas noches (after dark)*
Good night (farewell)	*Pase(n) buenas noches*
I am Doctor . . .	*Yo soy el Doctor . . .*
I don't speak Spanish.	*Yo no hablo español.*
I speak a little Spanish.	*Yo hablo un poco de español.*
Please	*Por favor*
Come in, Enter	*Pase, Entre*
Come here	*Venga acá*
Thank you	*Gracias*
Goodbye	*Adiós*
Go with God	*Vaya con Dios*
Go well	*Que le vaya bien*
Take care of yourself	*Cuídese bien*

Be careful!	*¡Cuidado!*
Again	*Otra vez*
Please repeat	*Repita, por favor*
Sit down	*Siéntese*
Lie down	*Acuéstese*
Stand up	*Levántese, Póngase de pie*
What did you say?	*¿Mande? ¿Cómo? ¿Qué dijo?*
Tell me	*Dígame*
Listen (to me)	*Escuche(me)*
Fast	*Rápido*
Slow	*Despacio*
Up	*Arriba*
Down	*Abajo*
Wait here, please	*Espérese aquí, por favor*
Just a minute	*Un momento*
Excuse me	*Con permiso, Dispénseme*
I'll be right back	*Ahorita vengo*
Everything is OK	*Todo está bien*
Everything will be OK	*Todo va a estar bien*
Calm down	*Cálmese*
Relax	*Descanse [No se apure]*†
Relax (physically)	*Relájese*°

†Southwestern localism
°Not used in New Mexico where it means "get embarrassed."

Don't worry	*No se preocupe [No se apure, No se apene]*†
Please take off your clothes and put on this gown.	*Por favor, quítese la ropa y póngase este camisón.*
Please call a (the) doctor.	*Por favor, llame un (al) doctor.*
I'm going to take your pulse.	*Voy a tomar su pulso.*
I'm going to take your blood pressure.	*Voy a tomar su presión arterial (presión de sangre).*
A little	*Poco, Un poco*
A lot, Much	*Mucho*
Today	*Hoy*
Yesterday	*Ayer*
Tomorrow°	*Mañana*
Do you have insurance	*¿Tiene usted seguros?*
What kind?	*¿Qué clase?*
Do you have a card from your insurance company?	*¿Tiene usted una tarjeta de su compañía de seguros?*
Sign here please.	*Firme aquí, por favor.*

†Southwestern localism

°*La mañana* means morning; e.g., *En la mañana yo camino una media hora.* (In the morning I walk for half an hour.)

2

Everyday Questions and Answers

These everyday questions and answers may be used for obtaining general information for the patient's record as well as for general conversation.

What is your name?	*¿Cómo se llama usted?*
My name is . . .	*Me llamo . . .*
Who is your doctor?	*¿Quién es su médico?*
	¿Cómo se llama su médico?
Doctor . . .	*El Doctor . . .*
	Se llama Doctor . . .
Have you seen another doctor or native healer for this problem?	*¿Ha visto a otro médico o curandero tocante a este problema (por este problema)?*
Yes, No	*Sí, No*
Do you speak English (Spanish)?	*¿Habla usted inglés (español)?*
Yes, No, A little	*Sí, No, Un poco*
Do you understand me?	*¿Me comprende? ¿Me entiende?*
Do you understand the instructions?	*¿Entiende las instrucciones?*
Yes, No, A little	*Sí, No, Un poco*
How old are you?	*¿Cuántos años tiene usted?*
I am twenty-five years old.	*Tengo veinticinco años.*

4

How old is she (he)?	¿Cuántos años tiene ella (él)?
She (he) is four months.	Ella (él) tiene cuatro meses.
I don't know.	Yo no sé.
Very old.	Muy viejo, -a. Muchos años.
Very young.	Muy joven. Pocos años.
When were you born?	¿Cuándo nació usted?
What year?	¿Qué año?
What month?	¿Qué mes?
What day?	¿Qué día?
I was born October 15, 1943.	Yo nací el quince de octubre, mil novecientos cuarenta y tres ("cuarentitrés").°
How are you?	¿Cómo está usted?
I am fine.	Estoy bien. Me siento bien.
I am sick.	Estoy enfermo, -a.
I am weak.	Estoy débil.
I am tired.	Estoy cansado, -a.
I feel bad.	Estoy malo, -a.°°
Where do you live?	¿Dónde vive usted?
In what state?	¿En qué estado?
In what city?	¿En qué ciudad?

°Note: The literal translation is "the fifteen of October, one thousand nine hundred and forty-three."

°°Note: *Soy malo, -a* means "I am a bad person."

On what street?	*¿En qué calle?*
What number?	*¿Qué número?*
I live at 385 Atrisco, SE.	*Yo vivo (habito) en el trescientos ochenta y cinco ("ochenticinco"), Atrisco, sureste.*
What do you do (job)?	*¿Qué es su oficio? ¿Cuál es su oficio?*
	¿Qué hace usted?
	¿Qué trabajo hace usted?
I work for the city.	*Yo trabajo por la ciudad.*
I work in a factory.	*Trabajo en una fábrica.*
I am a farmer.	*Soy ranchero (campesino)(finguero).*
I don't have a job.	*No tengo trabajo.*
Who else lives at home?	*¿Qué otras personas viven en su casa? ¿Quién más vive en su casa?*
Johnny, my son.	*Johnny, mi hijo.*
My father, mother	*Mi padre, madre*
My children, cousins	*Mis niños, primos*
My grandparents	*Mis abuelos*
My husband, man	*Mi esposo, hombre, marido*
My wife, woman	*Mi esposa, mujer*
My mother-in-law, father-in-law	*Mi suegra, -o*
My sister-in-law, brother-in-law	*Mi cuñada, -o*
My aunt, uncle	*Mi tía, -o*

Are you married?	*¿Es usted casado, -a?*
single?	*¿soltero, -a?*
divorced?	*¿divorciado, -a?*
widowed?	*¿viudo, -a?*
Yes, No	*Sí, No.*
What is your telephone number?	*¿Cuál es su número de teléfono?*
277-5129	*Dos, siete, siete, cinco, uno, dos, nueve.* °
Whom can we call?	*¿A quién podemos llamar?*
At what number?	*¿A qué número?*
Have you been here before?	*¿Ha estado usted aquí antes?*
Never	*Nunca*
Once	*Una vez*
Many times	*Muchas veces*
A week ago	*Hace una semana*
A long time ago	*Hace mucho tiempo*
Can you hear me?	*¿Puede usted oírme?*
Yes, No	*Sí, No*
If you speak in a loud voice.	*Si usted habla en voz alta.*

°Note: The above names each number separately. Another way is to group the last six numbers: two, seventy-seven, fifty-one, twenty-nine. *Dos, setenta y siete, cincuentiuno, veintinueve.*

3

Workups: Questions, Answers, and Phrases Relating to Major Common Complaints.

Following are a few brief questions, answers, and phrases helpful in obtaining histories and performing physical examination of patients in an emergency room, a clinic, or a doctor's office. Each section covers the workup of a major common complaint. Each is somewhat self-contained, so some phrases are repeated from section to section. Phrases common to many workups are listed in sections 1 and 2.

1. Phrases Common to Many Workups

When did this happen to you?	*¿Cuándo le pasó esto?*
Two hours ago	*Hace dos horas*
Five days ago	*Hace cinco días*
Three weeks ago	*Hace tres semanas*
Two months ago	*Hace dos meses*
A long time ago	*Hace mucho tiempo*
How long have you had this pain?	*¿Cuánto tiempo ha tenido usted este dolor?*
For six hours	*Por seis horas*
For nine days	*Por nueve días*
For one week	*Por una semana*
For four months	*Por cuatro meses*
For a long time	*Por mucho tiempo*
Since this morning	*Desde esta mañana*
Since last night	*Desde anoche*

About a week	*Más o menos una semana*
About (six) hours	*Unas (seis) horas*
Stand up	*Póngase de pie, Levántese, Párese*
Sit down	*Siéntese*
Lie down	*Acuéstese*
You must rest in bed.	*Tiene que descansar en cama.*
Are you hot? (Do you feel hot?)	*¿Tiene calor?* °
Are you cold? (Do you feel cold?)	*¿Tiene frío?* °
Do you have a fever?	*¿Tiene usted fiebre (calentura)?*
Has he (she) been drinking?	*¿Ha estado tomando alcohol (alcol)?*
He (she) is drunk.	*El (ella) está borracho, -a.*
I need a bedpan.	*Yo necesito un basín.*
Do you have any allergies?	*¿Tiene usted alergias? ¿Es usted alérgico, -a?*
Do any medicines make you sick?	*¿Hay medicinas que le hacen mal?*
Have you had penicillin before?	*¿Ha tomado usted penicilina antes (en el pasado)?*
Do you have high blood pressure?	*¿Tiene usted alta presión arterial (alta presión de sangre)?*
Do you take any medicines now?	*¿Toma usted medicinas ahora?*
You will need a blood test.	*Va a necesitar un examen de sangre.*
You will need an x-ray.	*Va a necesitar una radiografía (x-ray).*
Do you have any questions?	*¿Tiene usted algunas preguntas?*

° Note: *Está caliente* and *está frío* are in some places vulgar.

2. Prescription Phrases

A. Directions

I'm going to give you (prescribe) some pills, tablets, capsules,
     suppositories.
Le voy a dar (recetar) unas píldoras, tabletas, cápsulas, unos supositorios.

Use a suppository every six hours.
Use un supositorio cada seis horas.

Take three teaspoonsful (tablespoonsful) every two hours.
Tome tres cucharaditas (cucharas grandes) cada dos horas.

Take these pills four times a day for ten days.
Tome estas píldoras (pastillas) cuatro veces al día por diez días.

Use these drops as directed.
Use estas gotas como dice allí.

B. Times

Before (after) each meal.
Antes (después) de cada comida.

Before: bedtime, breakfast, lunch, dinner, eating.
Antes de: acostarse, desayunarse, almorzar, cenar, comer. °

At 9 o'clock in the morning.   *A las nueve de la mañana.*

At 3 o'clock in the afternoon.   *A las tres de la tarde.*

 At 7 o'clock in the evening.   *A las siete de la noche.*

°Note: In New Mexico, breakfast is *almuerzo*, lunch is *comida de medio día*.

3. After a Major Accident

Were you unconscious?	*¿Se desmayó? Estuvo desmayado, -a?*
For how long?	*¿Por cuánto tiempo?*
I don't know.	*No sé.*
Does anything hurt?	*¿Le duele algo?*
Where? Show me.	*¿Dónde? Enséñeme.*
Does it hurt when I press here?	*¿Le duele aquí cuando le aprieto?*
Do you know where you are?	*¿Sabe usted donde está?*
You are in the hospital.	*Usted está en el hospital.*
What day is today?	*¿Qué día es hoy?*
What month is it?	*¿Qué mes es?*
I'm going to start these fluids in your vein.	*Voy a ponerle estos fluidos (este líquido) en la vena.*
You will feel a little stick.	*Le va a doler un poquito. Va a sentir un piquete.*
Take a deep breath.	*Respire hondo (profundamente).*
You will be OK.	*Usted va a estar bien.*
You will need an operation.	*Usted va a necesitar una operación.*
I am calling the specialist to see you.	*Voy a llamar a un especialista que le vea.*

4. After a Minor Accident

How did this happen?	*¿Cómo pasó esto?*
How long ago?	*¿Hace cuánto tiempo?*
Does it hurt much?	*¿Le duele mucho?*
You will be OK.	*Usted va a estar bien.*
You will (won't) need stitches (sutures).	*(No) va a necesitar costuras (suturas) (puntos).*
I will put on medicine to make the pain go away.	*Le voy a poner medicina para quitarle el dolor.*
It will not hurt.	*No le va a doler.*
When was your last tetanus shot?	*¿Cuándo fué su última inyección (vacuna) contra el tétano?*
How did you burn yourself?	*¿Cómo se quemó?*
Lard, stove, hot water, fire, lye, acid	*Manteca, estufa (horno), agua caliente, fuego [lumbre],† lejia, ácido*
Tell me if this hurts.	*Dígame si le duele esto.*
You must keep it clean at all times.	*Tiene que tenerla (mantenerla) limpia todo el tiempo.*
I want to check it again in five days.	*Quiero examinarla otra vez en cinco días.*

†Southwestern localism

5. Headache

How long have you had the headache?	*¿Por cuánto tiempo ha tenido el dolor de cabeza?*
See phrases in section 1.	
Show me where it hurts.	*Enséñeme donde le duele.*
Is it throbbing or is it steady?	*¿Le dan pulsadas (Le palpita) o es constante?*
Throbbing	*Pulsando (palpitando)*
Steady	*Constante*
Does your neck hurt?	*¿Le duele el cuello (la nuca)?*
Yes, No, Sometimes	*Sí, No, A veces (De vez en cuando)*
Have you vomited?	*¿Ha vomitado usted? ¿Ha tenido vómitos?*
Is anything else hurting?	*¿Le duele algo más?*
Where?	*¿Dónde?*
Have you been feeling depressed?	*Ha estado usted deprimido, -a (triste)?*
Look at my finger.	*Mire mi dedo.*
Look at this.	*Mire esto.*
Keep looking here (there).	*Siga mirando aquí (allá).*
Look up.	*Mire para arriba.*
Look down.	*Mire para abajo.*
How many fingers do you see?	*¿Cuántos dedos ve usted?*
Squeeze my fingers.	*Apriéteme los dedos.*
Do this.	*Haga esto.*

You are OK.	*Usted está bien.*
I'm going to give you medicine.	*Le voy a dar medicina.*
Come back if you don't feel better.	*Regrese (vuelva) otra vez si no se siente mejor.*
I want to check your spinal fluid to look for infection.	*Quiero examinarle el líquido espinal para estar seguro que no tiene infección.*
For a spinal tap (to draw out spinal fluid), we need your written permission.	*Para una horadación espinal (para sacarle líquido espinal), necesitamos su permiso por escrito.*

6. Eye Complaints

Does your eye hurt?	*¿Le duele el ojo?*
My eye hurts.	*Me duele el ojo.*
Do your eyes hurt?	*¿Le duelen los ojos?*
My eyes hurt.	*Me duelen los ojos.*
Which one?	*¿Cuál?*
Left, right, both.	*Izquierdo, derecho, los dos (ambos).*
Did anything get in your eyes (metal, liquid)?	*¿Entró en sus ojos algo (metal, líquido)? ¿Le entró algo en los ojos?*
Did it affect your vision?	*¿Le afectó la vista?*
When you woke up this morning, were your eyes stuck together?	*¿Cuando se levantó esta mañana, tenía los ojos pegados?*
Cover one eye.	*Tápese un ojo.*
Read the letters.	*Lea las letras.*
Can you read this?	*¿Puede usted leer esto?*
Look at my finger.	*Mire mi dedo.*
Look at the (red) light.	*Mire la luz (colorada, roja).*
Look up.	*Mire para arriba.*
Look down.	*Mire para abajo.*
Look to the right.	*Mire para la derecha.*
Look to the left.	*Mire para la izquierda.*
You have something in your eye.	*Usted tiene algo en el ojo.*
I'm going to try to get it out.	*Voy a tratar de quitarlo.*

I'm going to put some medicine in your eye.	*Voy a ponerle medicina en el ojo.*
The medicine will burn for a moment; then it will feel better.	*La medicina le va a quemar (arder) por un momento; luego se va a sentir mejor.*
I will put a patch on your eye.	*Le voy a poner un parche sobre el ojo.*
Leave it on for 24 hours.	*Déjeselo por veinticuatro horas.*
I want to check your eye again tomorrow.	*Quiero examinarle el ojo otra vez mañana.*
You have an infection in your eye.	*Usted tiene una infección en el ojo.*
Put two drops of this medicine in your eyes four times a day for five days.	*Póngase (Echese) dos gotas de esta medicina en los ojos cuatro veces al día por cinco días.*

7. Earache

Does your ear hurt?	*¿Le duele el oído?*
Yes, my ear hurts.	*Sí, me duele el oído.*
Which one?	*¿Cuál?*
Left, right, both.	*Izquierdo, derecho, los dos (ambos).*
Is it itchy?	*¿Siente comezón? ¿Siente picazón?*
Does it feel plugged up (congested)?	*¿Se siente tapado?*
Does this hurt?	*¿Le duele esto?*
Are you deaf in this ear?	*¿Está usted sordo, -a en este oído?*
Have you put anything in your ear?	*¿No se ha puesto nada en el oído?*
You have an infection.	*Usted tiene una infección.*
I will give you some pills for the pain, infection.	*Le voy a dar unas píldoras para el dolor, la infección.*
I will give you ear drops.	*Le voy a dar gotas para el oído.*

8. Toothache

I have a toothache.	*Tengo dolor de muela.*
Open your mouth.	*Abra la boca.*
Which tooth hurts?	*¿Cuál diente le duele?*
Please point.	*Apunte, por favor.*
You have an abscess (infection).	*Usted tiene una postemilla (infección).*
You must go to a dentist (soon).	*Tiene que ir a un dentista (pronto).*
I will give you some pills for the pain, infection.	*Le voy a dar unas píldoras para el dolor, la infección.*

9. Sore Throat

Does your throat hurt?	*¿Le duele la garganta?*
Yes, my throat hurts.	*Sí, me duele la garganta.*
Is it painful or just scratchy?	*¿Le duele o está nomás rascosa (rasposa) (o sólo le arde)?*
Does it hurt to swallow?	*¿Le duele para tragar?*
Do you have a cold also?[*]	*Tiene catarro también? Está resfriado, -a también?*
Open your mouth.	*Abra la boca.*
Say "Ah."	*Diga "A."*
I am going to take a test (sample) for the laboratory.	*Voy a tomar una muestra (prueba) para el laboratorio.*
You need an injection of penicillin.	*Usted necesita una inyección de penicilina.*
Gargle with this medicine for the pain.	*Haga gárgaras con esta medicina para el dolor.*
Take these pills three times daily for a week.	*Tome estas píldoras tres veces al día por una semana.*

---

[*]Notes: *Constipado* can mean either to have a cold or to be constipated.

10. Cough

I have a bad cough.	*Tengo una mala tos.*
How long have you had the cough?	*¿Por cuánto tiempo ha tenido la tos?*
Does any sputum (phlegm) come up?	*¿Le sale flema (esputo)?*
What color is it?	*¿Qué color es?*
Clear, white, yellow, green.	*Clara, blanca, amarilla, verde.*
Have you coughed up any blood?	*¿Ha tosido usted sangre?*
Streaks of blood or clots?	*¿Rayas (líneas) de sangre o cuajarones? ¿Manchas de sangre o coágulos?*
Do you smoke cigarettes?	*¿Fuma usted cigarrillos (cigarros)?*
How many per day?	*¿Cuántos al día?*
One pack, more or less.	*Un paquete, más o menos.*
For how many years?	*¿Por cuántos años?*
Have you had tuberculosis, asthma, emphysema?	*¿Ha tenido usted tuberculosis (tisis), asma, enfisema?*
You have pneumonia.	*Usted tiene pulmonía, neumonía.*
We must treat you in (admit you to) the hospital.	*Tenemos que tratarle en el (admitirle al) hospital.*
Breathe deeply through your mouth.	*Respire hondo por la boca.*
Now relax.	*Ahora descanse.*
Relax.	*Descanse.*

11. Chest Pain

Where do you feel the pain?	*¿Dónde siente el dolor?*
Point to where it hurts.	*Apunte, por favor, a donde le duele.*
Did it stay in one place?	*¿Se quedó en un lugar?*
Do you still feel it?	*¿Lo siente todavía?*
How long did it last?	*¿Cuánto le duró?*
More than half an hour?	*¿Más de media hora?*
Did it travel to your jaw, shoulder, arm?	*¿Le pasó a la quijada, al hombro, al brazo?*
Was it dull and crushing like someone standing on your chest?	*¿Fué sordo y oprimido como si alguien estuviera colocado sobre su pecho?*
Was it sharp?	*¿Fué agudo?*
Have you had it before?	*¿Lo ha tenido antes?*
Do you have a heart condition?	*¿Tiene usted problemas del corazón?*
Do you take heart medicine?	*¿Toma usted medicina para el corazón?*
nitroglycerin?	*¿nitroglicerina?*
digitalis?	*¿digital?*
water pills?	*¿píldoras para sacar el agua?*
pills that you put under your tongue?	*¿píldoras que se ponen debajo de la lengua?*
Have you had a heart attack?	*¿Ha tenido usted ataque de corazón?*
Were you short of breath?	*¿Estuvo usted corto, -a de respiración?*

Did you perspire (sweat) when the pain came?	*¿Sudó usted cuando le vino el dolor?*
Did you pass out?	*¿Se desmayó usted?*
Have you hurt your chest in an accident recently?	*¿Se ha lastimado el pecho en un accidente últimamente?*
Have you had a cough?	*¿Ha tenido usted tos?*
Have you coughed up any blood?	*¿Ha tosido usted sangre?*
Streaks of blood or clots?	*¿Rayas (líneas) de sangre o cuajarones? (Manchas de sangre o coágulos?)*
Does it hurt when I press here?	*¿Le duele cuando le aprieto aquí?*
Breathe deeply through your mouth.	*Respire hondo por la boca.*
Does it hurt when you breathe?	*¿Le duele al respirar?*
I must start these fluids (liquids) in your vein.	*Tengo que ponerle estos fluidos (líquidos) en la vena.*
You will feel a little stick (pain).	*Va a sentir un poco de dolor (un piquetito).*
Hold still, please.	*No se mueva, por favor.*
This is oxygen.	*Esto es oxígeno.*

12. Gastro-Intestinal Problems

Abdominal pain	*El dolor de estómago*
Nausea	*La náusea (basca)*
Vomiting	*El vómito*
Diarrhea	*La diarrea (el torzón)*
How long have you had this pain?	*¿Por cuánto tiempo ha tenido este dolor?*
Can you hold down water without vomiting?	*¿Puede detener agua sin vomitarla?*
Where is the pain now?	*¿Dónde está el dolor ahora?*
Where was the pain when it started?	*¿Dónde estaba el dolor cuando comenzó?*
Please point there with one finger.	*Por favor, apunte allá con un dedo.*
Are you hungry (thirsty) now?	*¿Tiene usted hambre (sed) ahora?*
Relax, please.	*Descanse, por favor.*
Does it hurt when I press here?	*¿Le duele cuando le aprieto aquí?*
Does it hurt when I let go?	*¿Le duele cuando le suelto?*
Where?	*¿Dónde?*
What makes the pain go away?	*¿Qué alivia el dolor?*
What makes the pain worse?	*¿Qué empeora el dolor?*
Does eating food (drinking milk) make the pain better?	*¿Alivia el dolor comer (tomar leche)?*
Does eating make the pain worse?	*¿Empeora el dolor cuando come?*
Is there any position that makes the pain better? Lying down? Sitting forward? Sitting up?	*¿Hay alguna posición que alivia el dolor? ¿Acostarse? ¿Sentarse hacia adelante? ¿Sentarse recto?*

I need a sample of urine.	*Necesito una muestra de orina.*
Have you vomited blood?	*¿Ha vomitado usted sangre?*
I need to examine your rectum (anus).	*Necesito examinarle el recto (el ano).*
Have you noticed blood in your stools, or in the toilet water?	*¿Ha notado sangre en el excremento (la caca*) o en el agua del baño?*
Are your stools black like tar?	*¿Ha tenido excremento (caca*) (pase del cuerpo) negro (negra)?*
Do you drink?	*¿Acostumbra tomar? ¿Toma usted alcohol, alcol?*
For how long?	*¿Por cuánto tiempo?*
Have you been drinking beer, wine, whiskey? (Implies just recently.)	*¿Ha estado tomando usted cerveza, vino, "whiskey"?*
Have you had an ulcer?	*¿Ha tenido una úlcera?*
Do you take medicine for your stomach?	*¿Toma usted medicina para el estómago?*
What kind?	*¿Cómo se llama?*
Have you had operations (appendix, gallbladder)?	*¿Ha tenido operaciones (el apéndice, la hiel)? ¿Lo han operado—apéndice, vesícula biliar?*
Do you use drugs (a needle)?	*¿Usa usted drogas (una aguja)?*

---

*Note: May be considered vulgar outside the hospital setting, but is better understood by children.

13. Back Pain

How did you hurt yourself?

¿Cómo se lastimó?

I fell.

Me caí.

In a car accident.

En un accidente de carro (coche).

When did you hurt yourself?

¿Cuándo se lastimó?

Bend like this.

Agáchese (dóblese) así.

Does that (this) hurt?

¿Le duele eso (esto)?

I want you to rest in bed.

Quiero que usted descanse en cama.

I want you to apply heat to your back.

Quiero que le aplique calor a la espalda.

I will give you some pills for pain.

Le voy a dar unas píldoras para el dolor.

I want you to return in one week to see Dr. . . . , the bone specialist in the orthopedic clinic.

Quiero que vuelva en una semana a ver al Doctor . . . , el especialista de los huesos en la clínica ortopédica.

14. Urinary Problems

Does it hurt when you urinate?	¿Le duele al orinar?
Does it burn when you urinate?	¿Le quema (arde) al orinar?
Have you been urinating more than usual?	¿Ha estado orinando más seguido que antes?
Do you have blood in your urine?	¿Tiene usted sangre en el orín (la orina)?
Does your urine leak involuntarily?	¿Se le sale el orín involuntariamente?
Have you had stones in your urine?	¿Ha tenido usted piedras en el orín (la orina)?
Have you ever had kidney stones?	¿Ha tenido usted piedras en los riñones alguna vez?
Do you have pain in your back?	¿Tiene usted dolor de espalda?
Have you ever had a kidney (urinary) infection?	¿Ha tenido usted una infección en los riñones (urinaria) alguna vez?
Was it treated (this infection)?	¿Fué tratada (esta infección)?

15. Venereal Disease

Do you have a discharge from your penis (vagina)?

¿Tiene usted un desecho (descargo) de su pene (vagina)? ¿Le sale algo por el pene (la vagina)?

Does it hurt to urinate?

¿Le duele al orinar?

How long has this been going on?

¿Por cuánto tiempo ha tenido (pasado) esto?

Have you had it before?

¿Lo ha tenido antes?

Was it (were you) treated by a doctor?

¿Fué tratado (usted) por un doctor?

Do any joints (wrist, ankle, knee) hurt?

¿Le duelen las coyunturas—de la muñeca, del tobillo, de la rodilla?

Did it (you) get better?

¿Se mejoró (usted)?

Have you had any sores on your penis (in or around your vagina)?

¿Ha tenido usted llagas (úlceras) en su pene (en o alrededor de su vagina)?

Have you had any rash on your body?

¿Ha tenido usted sarpullido en el cuerpo?

Have you slept with a woman (man) recently?

¿Ha tenido relaciones sexuales con una mujer (un hombre) últimamente?

You must go to the Public Health Clinic.

Usted tiene que ir a la Clínica de Salud Pública.

16. Vaginal Discharge

How long has the discharge been there?

¿Por cuánto tiempo le ha estado desechando (saliendo esta descarga)?

Is your vagina itchy?

¿Tiene usted comezón en la vagina?

Have you had it before?

¿Lo ha tenido antes?

I must do a pelvic examination to check for an infection.

Tengo que hacer un examen pélvico para estar seguro que no tiene infección.

Please put on this gown.

Por favor, póngase este camisón.

Tell me if anything hurts.

Dígame si le duele algo.

I will go slowly.

Voy a hacerlo despacio.

Relax.

Descanse.

Breathe deeply.

Respire hondo (profundamente).

I will give you some medicine (cream, vaginal suppositories).

Le voy a dar medicina (crema, supositorios vaginales).

I need a urine sample.

Yo necesito una muestra de orina.

The bathroom is here (there).

El baño (privado) está aquí (allá).

Have you ever had venereal disease (V.D.)?

¿Ha tenido jamás (alguna vez) una enfermedad venérea (V.D.)?

17. Pregnancy

Are you pregnant?	*¿Está usted embarazada (enferma de niño, en cinta)?*
When was your last period?	*¿Cuándo fué su último periodo (tiempo) (última regla)?*
When is your baby due?	*¿Cuando va a llegar el niño?*
Have you had any infections like German measles (rubella fever) during this pregnancy?	*¿Ha tenido algunas infecciónes como, por ejemplo, el sarampión de tres días (rubeola) durante el embarazo?*
Have you been using any medications?	*¿Ha estado tomando algunas medicinas?*
What kind?	*¿Qué clase?*
What is the name?	*¿Cómo se llaman?*
Can you bring them to me?	*¿Me las puede traer?*
Have you been taking narcotics during this pregnancy?	*¿Ha estado tomando drogas durante el embarazo?*
Have you been drinking regularly (daily) during this pregnancy?	*¿Ha tomado alcohol regularmente (todos los días) durante el embarazo?*
Do you have diabetes?	*¿Tiene usted diabetes?*
Do you have high blood pressure?	*¿Tiene usted alta presión arterial?*
How many times have you been pregnant?	*¿Cuántas veces ha estado embarazada (en cinta)?*
Have you had any miscarriages?	*¿Ha tenido usted algún malparto (abortos involuntarios)?*
Have you had any abortions?	*¿Ha tenido usted abortos voluntarios?*
How many children do you have now?	*¿Cuántos niños tiene usted ahora?*

How many?	*¿Cuántos?*
Have your labor pains started?	*¿Le han empezado los dolores?*
How many minutes apart are they?	*¿Cuántos minutos entre uno y otro?*
Has your water broken?	*¿Se le ha quebrado el agua (la fuente)?*
Have you had any vaginal bleeding?	*¿Se ha sangrado usted? ¿Le ha salido sangre por la vagina?*
Have you had a severe headache?	*¿Ha tenido usted fuerte dolor de cabeza?*

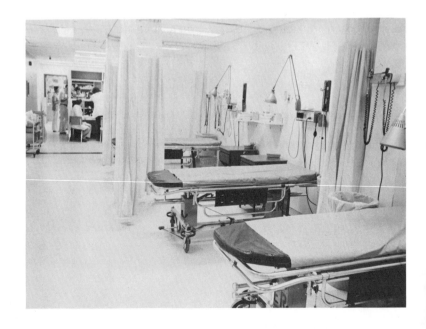

18. Pain Of An Extremity

How did you hurt yourself?	*¿Cómo se lastimó usted?*
I fell down.	*Me caí.*
I was hit with a stick, stone, fist.	*Me pegaron con un palo, una piedra, la mano (el puño).*
He hit me.	*Me dió un golpe. Me pegó.*
I was cut with a knife.	*Me cortaron con un cuchillo (una navaja, una daga, un puñal).*
I was shot with a gun.	*Me dieron un balazo.* °
Move your fingers, toes, elbow, wrist, knee, ankle.	*Mueva sus dedos, dedos del pie, (su) codo, muñeca, rodilla, tobillo.*
Do you feel this?	*¿Siente usted esto?*
Is it (the pain) sharp or dull?	*¿Es agudo o sordo (el dolor)?*
Is your arm (leg) weak?	*¿Está débil su brazo (pierna)?*
Close your eyes.	*Cierre los ojos.*
How many points do you feel?	*¿Cuántas puntas (piquetes) siente usted?*
The bone specialist (orthopedist) will see you.	*El especialista de los huesos (ortopedista) le va a ver.*
He will be here in a few minutes.	*El viene en unos minutos.*
You have a pulled muscle.	*Usted tiene un músculo jalado (rasgado).*
You have a broken bone.	*Usted tiene un hueso quebrado.*
You have a sprained	*Usted tiene un, -a . . . torcido, -a*
Your shoulder is dislocated.	*Su hombro está dislocado (jalado).*

°Note: Literally: They gave me a gun shot.

You will need a cast (bandage) (sling).	*Usted va a necesitar un yeso (envoltura, vendaje) (banda, cabestrillo).*
You have a sprained ankle.	*Usted tiene el tobillo torcido.*
You will need to see an orthopedist again in three days.	*Tiene que ver al ortopedista en tres días otra vez.*

19. Rashes

How long have you had the rash?	*¿Por cuánto tiempo ha tenido usted el sarpullido?*
Has an insect bitten you?	*¿Le ha picado un insecto?*
spider?	*¿una araña?*
bee?	*¿una abeja?*
wasp?	*¿una avispa?*
scorpion?	*¿un alacrán (un escorpión)?*
snake (nonpoisonous)	*¿una culebra (serpiente) (no venenosa)?*
rattlesnake?	*¿una víbora (culebra de cascabel)?*
Have you eaten anything different lately?	*¿Ha comido usted algo diferente últimamente?*
Have you used a new soap lately— for yourself or your clothes?	*¿Ha usado usted un jabón nuevo últimamente—para usted mismo o su ropa?*
Is it itchy?	*¿Le da comezón?*
Does it hurt?	*¿Le duele?*
Where else do you have the rash?	*¿En qué otra parte tiene usted el sarpullido?*
Have you had this before?	*¿Ha tenido usted esto antes?*
You have an infection.	*Usted tiene una infección.*
You have an allergy.	*Usted tiene una alergia.*
I will give you a cream.	*Le voy a dar una crema.*
I will give you some pills.	*Le voy a dar unas píldoras.*

20. Overdose/Poisoning

Overdose

Did he (she) take some pills?   *¿Tomó él (ella) pastillas (píldoras),*
capsules?   *cápsulas?*

Did he (she) inject something?   *¿Se inyectó con algo?*

Did he (she) inject heroin?   *¿Se inyectó con heroina?*

Did he (she) take sleeping pills?   *¿Tomó él (ella) píldoras para*
                                 dormir?

What kind of pills did he (she) take?   *¿Qué clase de píldoras tomó?*

   sleeping pills?   *¿píldoras de dormir?*

   diet pills?   *¿píldoras de dieta?*

   tranquilizers?   *¿tranquilizantes (calmantes)?*

   many kinds?   *¿muchas clases?*

   different kinds?   *¿diferentes clases?*

What color were the pills?   *¿De qué color eran las píldoras?*

(See color terminology.)

What shape were the pills?   *¿De qué forma eran las píldoras?*

   round?   *¿redondas?*

   triangular?   *¿triangulares?*

   square?   *¿cuadradas?*

Were they large or small?   *¿Eran grandes o chicas (pequeñas)?*

How many did he (she) take?   *¿Cuántas tomó?*

I don't know.   *No sé.*

Many.   **Muchas.**

The whole bottle.	*Toda la botella (la botella entera).*
Do you have the bottle that the pills (liquid) came in?	*¿Tiene la botella de las píldoras, del líquido?*
Can you bring me the bottle that the pills (liquid) came in?	*¿Puede traerme la botella en la cual vinieron estas píldoras (este líquido)?*
It is very important!	*¡Esto es muy importante!*
Has he (she) vomited?	*¿Ha vomitado?*
Did he (she) vomit any pills?	*¿Vomitó píldoras?*
Have you given him (her) anything else to	*Le ha dado algo más para*
eat or drink?	*comer o beber?*
water?	*¿agua?*
milk?	*¿leche?*
tea?	*¿té?*
coffee?	*¿café?*
ipecac?	*¿ipecacuana?*
I am going to give you an injection.	*Le voy a dar una inyección.*
I must put this tube into your stomach, through your nose.	*Tengo que ponerle este tubo dentro del estómago, por la nariz.*
Relax!	*¡Cálmese!*
Swallow!	*¡Trágueselo!*
Drink this medicine.	*Tome esta medicina.*
Now drink this water.	*Ahora tome este agua.*
This medicine will make you vomit.	*Esta medicina le va a hacer vomitar.*

I must start these fluids in your veins.	*Tengo que darle estos fluidos (este líquido) por las venas.*
I want you to breathe this oxygen.	*Quiero que respire este oxígeno.*
You will have to stay in the hospital today (overnight).	*Va a tener que quedarse en el hospital hoy (esta noche).*

Poisoning

What did the child drink?	*¿Qué bebió el niño (la niña)?*
What did the child eat?	*¿Qué comió el niño (la niña)?*
kerosene	*kerosena, aceite de lámpara*
gasoline	*gasolina*
drain cleaner	*destapador de cañeria, limpiador de tuberia*
lye	*lejia*
bleach	*blanqueador*
paint thinner	*disolvente de pintura*
aspirin	*aspirina*
medicine	*medicina*
The child must stay in the hospital today (tonight).	*El niño (la niña) tiene que quedarse en el hospital hoy (esta noche).*

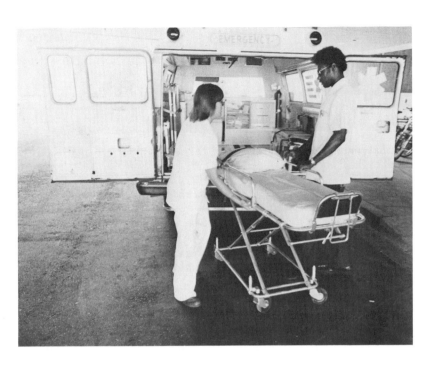

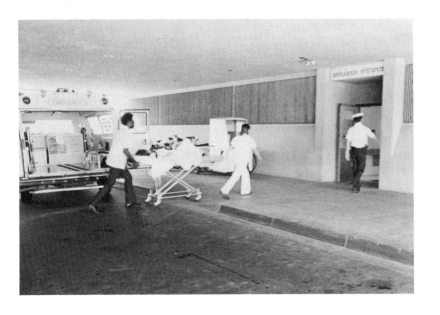

21. Unconscious patient

What happened to him (her)?	*¿Qué le pasó a él (ella)?*
He (she) fainted.	*Se desmayó.*
He (she) complained of pain and fell to the floor.	*Se quejó de dolor y se cayó al suelo.*
He (she) choked on food.	*Se ahogó con comida.*
He (she) got drunk.	*Se emborrachó.*
Has he (she) been drinking?	*¿Ha estado él (ella) tomando licor (alcol, alcohol)?*
Has he (she) heart disease?	*¿Tiene él (ella) enfermedad del corazón? ¿Está él (ella) enfermo, -a, del corazón?*
diabetes (sugar in the urine)?	*¿diabetes (azúcar en el orín)?*
emphysema?	*¿enfisema?*
bronchitis?	*¿bronquitis?*
breathing problems?	*¿dificultad al respirar?*
Is he (she) taking any medications?	*¿Está él (ella) tomando medicinas?*
What kind?	*¿Qué clase?*
For the heart?	*¿Para el corazón?*
For the lungs?	*¿Para los pulmones?*
Insulin?	*¿Insulina?*
Can you bring me the medicines that he (she) takes?	*¿Puede usted traerme las medicinas que él (ella) toma?*
Has he (she) had a recent head injury?	*¿Ha sufrido él (ella) una herida recientemente en la cabeza?*
Has he (she) vomited?	*¿Ha vomitado?*

Has he (she) been treated at the hospital, clinic, office before?	*¿Ha recibido tratamiento él (ella) en el hospital, la clínica, la oficina antes?*
Has he (she) been ill lately?	*¿Ha estado enfermo, -a, últimamente?*
Has he (she) been in the hospital recently?	*¿Ha estado él (ella) en el hospital recientemente?*
Is she pregnant?	*¿Está ella embarazada (en cinta)?*
Does he (she) have any allergies?	*¿Tiene él (ella) alergias?* °
Has he (she) been stung by a bee (or wasp)?	*¿Le picó a él (ella) una abeja (una avispa)?*
Was he (she) bitten by a snake?	*¿Le picó una víbora?*
What kind?	*¿Qué clase?*
We must check his (her) spinal fluid to look for the infection.	*Tenemos que examinarle el líquido espinal para buscar la infección.*
For a spinal tap (to draw out spinal fluid) we need your written permission.	*Para una horadación espinal, (para sacarle líquido espinal) necesitamos su permiso por escrito.*

°Note: If the word *alergias* is not understood, ask "*¿Le hace mal alguna comida o medicina?*"

22. Family Planning

This is a sensitive subject. Because of the large number of euphemisms and local terms, it is important to have much of the discussion conducted by a local Spanish-speaking person, preferably a female.

Are you interested in discussing birth control?	*¿Está usted interesada en hablar de la anticoncepción? (como evitar niños?)*
Do you know about birth control?	*¿Sabe usted de la anticoncepción?*
Are you married?	*¿Está usted casada?*
Do you prefer to discuss this with your husband or boyfriend?	*¿Prefiere usted hablar de esto con su esposo o su novio?*
Do you prefer to discuss this in the presence of your husband or boyfriend?	*¿Prefiere usted hablar de esto con su esposo o su novio presente?*
Are you interested in using some form of birth control?	*¿Está usted interesada en usar alguna forma de anticoncepción (de cuidarse)?*
Would you like to have more children?	*¿Quiere usted tener más niños?*
When?	*¿Cuándo?*
Soon	*Pronto*
Now	*Ahora*
In a few years	*Dentro de pocos años*
Never	*Nunca*
Do you know about . . .	*¿Sabe usted de . . .*
birth control methods	*métodos de anticoncepción (cuidarse) para no quedar en cinta?*
birth control pills	*píldoras de anticoncepción (anticonceptivas)?*

IUD	*el anillo, el lupo, el aparato (intra-uterino)?*
diaphragm	*el diafragma?*
foams	*espumas, jaleas?*
tubal ligation	*ligadura de los tubos, amarrada°?*
vasectomy	*vasectomia°°?*
Have you ever used . . .	*¿Ha usado usted alguna vez . . .*
Would you like to use . . .	*¿Quisiera usted usar . . .*
I will ask someone to discuss this with you in Spanish.	*Voy a pedirle a alguien que hable de esto con usted en español.*

°Note: Common expression meaning "tied."
°°Note: The translator should alert them to the fact that erection and ejaculation are not affected.

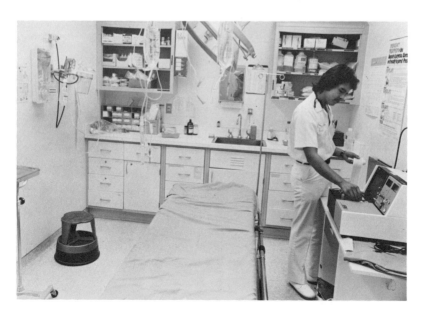

23. Common Pediatric Problems

A. Fever   *Fiebre (Calentura)* *

How long has he (she) had a fever?	*¿Cuanto tiempo hace que tiene fiebre (calentura)?*
Has he (she) had diarrhea or vomiting?	*¿Ha tenido diarrea o vómitos?*
Is he (she) taking fluids?	*¿Está tomando líquidos?*
Has he (she) had changes in his (her) behavior?	*¿Ha tenido cambios en su conducta?*
Is he (she) lethargic?	*¿Aletargado(a)?*
Irritable?	*¿Inquieto(a)?*
Poor feeding?	*¿Poco apetito?*
Seizures?	*¿Convulsiones? (ataques)*
Cough?	*¿Tos?*
Not playful?	*¿Desinteresado(a) en jugar?*
Does he (she) complain of headache or stiff neck?	*¿Se queja de dolor de cabeza o dolor de cuello?*
Is anyone else sick at home?	*¿Hay alguien otro enfermo en casa?*
at school?	*¿en la escuela?*
at the day care center?	*en la guardería infantil?*
We must check his blood, urine, and spinal fluid to look for the infection.	*Tenemos que examinarle la sangre, la orina, y el líquido espinal para buscar la infección.*
For a spinal tap (to draw out fluid) we need your written permission.	*Para una horadación espinal (para sacarle líquido espinal) necesitamos su permiso por escrito.*

*Fiebre vs. calentura: in some regions fiebre means a specific type of fever, e.g., yellow fever, typhoid fever, and the like. Calentura always means high temperature.

We must lower his (her) temperature.	*Tenemos que bajarle la temperatura.*
He (she) will have to stay here for a few hours.	*Tendrá que quedarse aquí por unas horas.*
We will have to admit him (her) to the hospital.	*Tendremos que admitirlo(la) al hospital.*
He (she) must take this medicine.	*Tiene que tomar esta medicina.*
Do you have a telephone or a number where I can call you?	*¿Tiene usted teléfono o un número donde yo le pueda llamar?*
Do you have a thermometer?	*¿Tiene usted un termómetro?*
Tylenol?	*¿Tylenol?*
aspirin?	*¿aspirina?*
Do you know how to use it?	*¿Sabe como usarlo?*
Please call us if:	*Por favor llamenos si:*
his (her) temperature goes up.	*su temperatura sube.*
his (her) temperature doesn't go down.	*su temperatura no baja.*
he (she) doesn't want to drink.	*no quiere beber nada.*
Put him (her) in a tub and sponge him (her) with warm water. Do not use alcohol.	*Póngalo(la) en el baño y bañalo(la) con agua tibia. No use alcohol.*

B. Vomiting
Diarrhea
Gastroenteritis

Vomitando
Diarrea
La Gastroenteritis

How long has he (she) had diarrhea?	*¿Cuanto tiempo hace que tiene diarrea?*

How many stools has he (she) had in the past 24 hours?	*¿Cuantas veces ha hecho caca en las últimas veinticuatro horas?*
Are the stools watery or just soft?	*¿Son las cacas como agua o solamente blandas?*
Have they been bloody or mucosy?	*¿Han sido sangrientas o mucosas?*
When was the last time he (she) urinated?	*¿Cuando fué la última vez que orinó?*
Was the diaper damp or soaked?	*¿Estaba el pañal húmedo o empapado?*
Is he (she) vomiting all the time or only when he eats?	*¿Está vomitando todo el tiempo o solo cuando come?*
Has he (she) had a fever?	*¿Ha tenido fiebre (calentura)?*
a cold?	*¿un resfriado?*
a head cold?	*¿un catarro?*
Is there anyone else at home who is sick?	*¿Hay alguien otro en casa que esta enfermo?*
has diarrhea?	*¿tiene diarrea?*
What have you been feeding him (her)	*¿Qué le ha estado dando para comer?*
The stomach is irritated.	*El estómago está irritado.*
His intestines are inflamed and need simple foods.	*Sus intestinos están inflamados y necesitan comidas livianas.*
We have to wait until the intestines heal by themselves.	*Tenemos que esperar a ver que los intestinos se recuperan solos.*
There is no medicine to help.	*No hay medicina que le ayude.*

We have to give him (her) fluids slowly so he (she) won't vomit.	*Tenemos que darle líquidos poco a poco para que no vomite.*
We must start an I.V. because he (she) is very dry (dehydrated).	*Tenemos que darle un suero por la vena porque está muy seco (deshidratado).* *seca (deshidratada).*
Give him clear liquids in small sips for 24 hours.	*Déle líquidos claros en traguitos pequeños por veinticuatro horas.*
Gatorade	*Gatorade*
Kool-aid	*Koolaid*
Jello	*gelatina*
Pedialyte	*pedialyte*
apple juice	*jugo de manzana*
flat soda pop	*soda sin gas*
Then (next) give him:	*Después déle:*
soy bean formula	*formula de soja (soya)*
bananas	*plátanos*
boiled rice	*arroz herbido*
rice cereal	*cereal de arroz*
apple sauce	*compota (puré) de manzana*
You shouldn't give him (her) any foods that are:	*No debe darle comidas:*
milk products	*de leche*
fried	*fritas*
greasy	*aceitosas*
spicy	*picantes (con especias)*

Please note how often he urinates.	*Por favor fíjese bien cada cuantes veces orina.*
Do you have a telephone or a number where I can call you?	*Tiene usted teléfono o un número donde yo le pueda llamar?*
Call me if he doesn't urinate in 8 hours.	*Llámeme si no orina en ocho horas.*
You should call me if:	*Usted debe llamarme si:*
he (she) continues to vomit.	*continua vomitando.*
the diarrhea worsens.	*la diarrea empeora.*
his (her) temperature goes up.	*su temperatura sube.*
Does anyone in the family work in a food-handling job?*	*¿Hay alguien en la familia que trabaja con alimentos?*
a cook?	*¿cocinero?*
a waiter?	*¿mesero? (mozo)*
a dishwasher?	*¿lavaplatos?*

C. Asthma

Asma

How long has he (she) had this wheezing?	*¿Cuanto tiempo hace que tiene este sonido asmático?*
Did it start suddenly or gradually?	*¿Le comenzó de repente o poco a poco?*
Has he (she) had (this) wheezing before?	*¿Ha tenido (este) sonido asmático antes?*
Does he take medicine for wheezing?	*¿Toma medicina para el sonido asmático?*

*If a family member is a food handler, you may want to get a translator to explain the need for strict hygiene.

All the time or just when wheezing?	¿Todo el tiempo o solo cuando tiene el sonido asmático?
What started the wheezing?	¿Como le comenzó el sonido asmático?
exercise?	¿ejercicio?
cold air?	¿aire frio?
dust?	¿polvo?
a cold?	¿un resfriado?
being upset?	¿cuando se molesta?
dogs?	¿perros?
cats?	¿gatos?
Has he (she) been vomiting?	¿Ha estado vomitando?
coughing?	tosiendo?
Has he (she) had a fever?	¿Ha tenido fiebre (calentura)
Did he (she) swallow something small?	¿Se tragó algo pequeño?
a peanut?	un maní (cacahuete)?
money (a coin?)	dinero (una moneda)?
Does he (she) have:	¿Tiene:
allergies?	¿alergias?
eczema?	¿eczema?
itchy skin?	¿comezón en la piel?
rash?	¿ronchas?

Does anyone else in the family have:	*¿Hay alguien otro en la familia con:*
allergies?	*¿alergias?*
eczema?	*¿eczema?*
itchy skin?	*¿comezón en la piel?*
rash?	*¿ronchas?*
We need to give him shots to help him (her) breathe better.	*Tenemos que darle inyecciones para ayudarle a respirar mejor.*
We need to give him (her) fluids and medicine intravenously.	*Tenemos que darle líquidos y medicina por la vena.*
He must take this medicine for _____days.	*Tiene que tomar esta medicina por _____dias.*
(See page 55 for numbers.)	
Please call us if he (she) continues:	*Por favor llamenos se continua:*
to vomit.	*vomitando.*
to have difficulty breathing.	*respirando con dificultad.*
We need to see him (her) again.	*Tenemos que verlo(la) otra vez.*
What kind of heating do you have in your house?	*¿Qué tipo de calefacción tiene en su casa?*
gas	*gas*
steam	*vapor*
coal	*carbón*
oil	*aceite*
electricity	*electricidad*

wood	*leña*
nothing (none)	*nada (ningún)*
You need to use a humidifier (a steam machine) at night.	*Tiene que usar un humedifacador (un aparato que hace vapor) por la noche.*
Don't let him (her) go outside.	*No lo (la) permita salir afuera de casa.*
Give him (her) lots of fluids.	*Déle muchos líquidos.*
tea	*té*
water	*agua*
ginger ale	*gingerale*
Seven-up	*Seven-up*
juice	*jugo*
clear liquids	*líquidos claros*

4

Terminology

1. Anatomical Terms

English-Spanish

abdomen	*el abdomen, estómago [la panza]*†
ankle	*el tobillo*
appendix	*el apéndice, la apendix [la tripita]*†
arm	*el brazo*
armpit	*el sobaco, la axila*
artery	*la arteria, vena*
back	*la espalda*
blood	*la sangre*
bone	*el hueso*
bowels	*los intestinos [las tripas]*†
breast(s)	*el pecho (los senos)*
cervix	*el cuello de la matriz*
cheek	*la mejilla, el cachete*
chest	*el pecho, tórax*
chin	*la barba, la piocha, el talache, la barbilla*
clavicle, collarbone	*la clavícula, cuenca*
coccyx	*la colita, coxis*
diaphragm	*la diafragma*
ear (inner)	*el oído, sentido*
ear (outer)	*la oreja*
elbow	*el codo*
esophagus	*el esófago*
eye	*el ojo*
eyelid	*el párpado*
face	*la cara*
fallopian tube	*el tubo falopio (trampa de falopio)*
finger	*el dedo*

fingernail	*la uña*
foot	*el pie*
gallbladder	*la hiel, vesícula biliar*
gland	*la glándula*
hair	*el pelo, cabello*
hand	*la mano*
head	*la cabeza*
heart	*el corazón*
heel	*el talón*
hip	*la cadera [el cuadril]* †
inguinal region	*el ingle [la aldilla],*† *la región inguinal*
intestines	*los intestinos [las tripas]* †
jaw	*la mandíbula, quijada*
joint	*la coyuntura, articulación*
kidney	*el riñon*
knee	*la rodilla*
larynx	*la laringe*
leg	*la pierna*
lip	*el labio*
liver	*el hígado*
lung	*el pulmón*
mouth	*la boca*
nail (finger or toe)	*la uña (dedo de la mano, del pie)*
neck	*el cuello, la nuca, el pescuezo*
nerve	*el nervio*
nose	*la nariz*
nostrils	*las narices (ventana de la nariz)*
ovary	*el ovario*
palm	*la palma*

†Southwestern localism

pancreas	*el páncreas*
patella	*el hueso de la rodilla*
pelvis	*la cadera*
penis	*el pene, miembro*
rectum	*el recto, ano*
rib	*la costilla*
scalp	*el casco, cuero cabelludo*
scapula	*la paleta, escápula, homóplato*
scrotum	*el escroto, la bolsa de los testículos*
shin	*la canilla, espinilla*
shoulder(s)	*el, los hombro(s)*
skin	*la piel, el cuero*
skull	*el cráneo*
spine	*el espinazo, la columna vertebral*
spleen	*el bazo*
sternum	*el hueso del pecho, esternón*
stomach	*el estómago [la panza]*†
tendon	*el tendón*
thigh	*el muslo*
throat	*la garganta*
thumb	*el dedo gordo, pulgar*
thyroid	*el tiroides*
toe	*el dedo del pie*
tongue	*la lengua*
tonsils	*las amígdalas, anginas*
trachea	*la traquea, el gaznate*
umbilicus	*el ombligo*
urine	*la orina, el orín*
urethra	*la uretra*
vagina	*la vagina*
vein	*la vena*
wrist	*la muñeca*

Spanish-English

las amígdalas	tonsils
la amigdalitis	tonsilitis
la angina	tonsil (or tonsilitis)
el apéndice [*la appendix*]†	appendix
la arteria	artery
la axila	armpit
la barba	beard
la barbilla	chin
la boca	mouth
[*el bofe*]†	lung
el brazo	arm
el cabello	hair
la cabeza	head
el cachete	cheek
la cadera	lower back (muscular), hip
la canilla	shin or calf
la cara	face
el cerebro	brain
la cintura	waist
la clavícula	collarbone
la columna vertebral	spine
el codo	elbow
el corazón	heart
la costilla	rib
la coyuntura	joint
el cuello	neck, collar
[*el cuadril*]	hip
la cuenca de los ojos	eye socket
el cuerpo	body
el dedo	finger
el dedo del pie	toe
el dedo gordo	thumb
el diente	tooth (incisor or bicuspid)
la espalda	back
la espinilla	shin (pimple or blackhead)

†Southwestern localism

el espinazo	spine
el estómago	stomach
la garganta	throat
la glándula	gland
el hígado	liver
el hombro	shoulder
el hueso	bone
los intestinos	intestines, bowels
el labio	lip
la lengua	tongue
la mandíbula	jaw
la mano	hand
la matriz	womb, pelvic area
la mejilla	cheek
la muela	tooth (molar)
la muñeca	wrist, doll
el músculo	muscle
el muslo	thigh
la nalga°	rump, buttock
la nariz	nose
el nervio	nerve
el oído	ear (inner)
el ojo	eye
la oreja	ear (outer)
la orina (*el orín*)	urine
el pecho	chest, breast
el pelo	hair
el pene	penis
la pierna	leg
el pulmón	lung
el pulgar (*dedo gordo*)	thumb

°Note: The plural *nalgas* is less polite.

el pulso	pulse
la quijada	jaw
el riñón	kidney
la rodilla	knee
la sangre	blood
el (los) seno(s)	chest, breasts; also womb
los sesos	brains
el sobaco	armpit
el talache	chin
el talón	heel
el tobillo	ankle
la tonsilitis	tonsilitis
[los tonsils]†	tonsils
[tripa]†	intestines, gut, bowels
[tripita]†	appendix
el útero	uterus
la vena	vein
la vejiga	bladder, blister

2. Numbers

Cardinals

0	*cero*	10	*diez*
1	*uno, una*	11	*once*
2	*dos*	12	*doce*
3	*tres*	13	*trece*
4	*cuatro*	14	*catorce*
5	*cinco*	15	*quince*
6	*seis*	16	*dieciséis*
7	*siete*	17	*diecisiete*
8	*ocho*	18	*dieciocho*
9	*nueve*	19	*diecinueve*

†Southwestern localism

20 *veinte*
21 *veintiuno*°
22 *veintidós*
23 *veintitrés*
30 *treinta*
31 *treintiuno (treinta y uno)*°
40 *cuarenta*
42 *cuarentidós (cuarenta y dos)*
50 *cincuenta*
54 *cincuenticuatro (cincuenta y cuatro)*
60 *sesenta*
68 *sesentiocho (sesenta y ocho)*
70 *setenta*
75 *setenticinco (setenta y cinco)*
80 *ochenta*
83 *ochentitrés (ochenta y tres)*
90 *noventa*
99 *noventinueve (noventa y nueve)*
100 *ciento (by itself, 100 is cien)*
101 *ciento uno*
125 *ciento veinticinco*
200 *doscientos*
245 *doscientos cuarenticinco*
300 *trescientos*
500 *quinientos*
1,000 *mil*
2,000 *dos mil*

Ordinals

first	*primero, -a*
second	*segundo, -a*
third	*tercero, -a*
fourth	*cuarto, -a*°°
fifth	*quinto, -a*
sixth	*sexto, -a*
seventh	*séptimo, -a*
eighth	*octavo, -a*

°Note: Either form is correct for all numbers.

°°Note: *Cuarto* also means room.

ninth	*noveno, -a*
tenth	*décimo, -a*
eleventh	*undécimo, -a*
twelfth	*duodécimo, -a*
thirteenth	*treceavo, -a*
fourteenth	*catorceavo, -a*
eighteenth	*décimo octavo, -a*
nineteenth	*décimo noveno, -a*
twentieth	*vigésimo, -a*
twenty-first	*vigésimo primero*
thirtieth	*trigésimo, -a*

3. Days of the Week*

Sunday	*domingo*
Monday	*lunes*
Tuesday	*martes*
Wednesday	*miércoles*
Thursday	*jueves*
Friday	*viernes*
Saturday	*sábado*

4. Months of the Year*

January	*enero*
February	*febrero*
March	*marzo*
April	*abril*
May	*mayo*
June	*junio*
July	*julio*
August	*agosto*
September	*septiembre, setiembre*
October	*octubre*
November	*noviembre*
December	*diciembre*

*Note: Days and months of the year are masculine. They do not require a capital letter.

5. Colors

blond	*rubio, güero*
black	*negro*
blue	*azul*
brown	*café, acafetado, moreno*
green	*verde*
gray	*gris*
pink	*rosa*
purple	*morado*
red	*rojo, colorado* (*tinto*—refers to wine)
white	*blanco*
yellow	*amarillo*

Vocabulary—Vocabulario

abdomen (n.)	*el abdomen, estómago*
abdominal (adj.)	*abdominal*
abortion (n.)	*el aborto*
accidental	*el malparto (aborto involuntario) (aborto accidental)*
induced	*el aborto (voluntario) (inducido)*
abrasion (n.)	*la rozadura, razpón*
abscess (n.)	*la hinchazón, el absceso*
of a tooth	*el absceso de un diente, la postemilla*
ache (n.)	*el dolor*
ache (v.)	*doler*
acidity (n.)	*las acedias, agruras*
heartburn	*acedias, agruras*
address (n.)	*la dirección, el domicilio*
afterbirth (n.)	*la placenta, el segundo parto*
again (adv.)	*otra vez, de nuevo*
against (prep.)	*contra*
age (n.)	*la edad*
alcohol (n.)	*el alcol, licor, alcohol*
ambulance (n.)	*la ambulancia*
anemic (adj.)	*anémico, -a*
anger (n.)	*el coraje, la cólera, la rabia*
anguish (n.)	*la congoja, angustia*
ankle (n.)	*el tobillo*
ankle bone (n.)	*el tobillo*
appendicitis (n.)	*la apendicitis, inflamación de la tripita*
appendix (n.)	*el apéndice, la tripita*

"La appendix" is used and understood in New Mexico.

appetite (n.)	*el apetito*
appointment (n.)	*la cita*
arm (n.)	*el brazo*
armpit (n.)	*el sobaco*
artery (n.)	*la arteria, vena*
arthritis (n.)	*la artritis*

aspirin (n.)	*la aspirina*
asthma (n.)	*el asma*
attack (n.)	*el ataque*
average (mean) (n.)	*el promedio*
baby (n.)	*el niño, la niña, el nene, la nena*
back (n.)	*la espalda*
bag of waters (n.)	*la bolsa de aguas*
bandage (n.)	*la envoltura, vendaje*
bath, bathroom (n.)	*el baño, cuarto de baño*
bathe (v.)	
another	*bañar*
oneself	*bañarse*
bed (n.)	*la cama*
bedbug (n.)	*la chinche*
bedpan (n.)	*el basín*
bee (n.)	*la abeja*
beer (n.)	*la cerveza*
belch (v.)	*regoldar, regurgitar*
bend over (v.)	*agacharse, doblarse*
bile (n.)	*la hiel, bilis*
birth (n.)	*el nacimiento*
birth control (pill) (n.)	*la anticoncepción (píldora de anticoncepción) (píldora anticonceptiva)*
birthmark (n.)	*la marca de nacimiento, lunar*
bite (n.)	
animal	*la mordida*
insect	*el piquete*
bladder (n.)	*la vejiga*
blanket (n.)	*la cobija, fresada, manta*
bleed (v.)	*sangrar*
blind (adj.)	*ciego, -a*
blink (v.)	*parpadear*
blister (n.)	*la ampolla, vejiga*
blood (n.)	*la sangre*
blood clot (n.)	*el cuajarón, coágulo*
blood pressure (n.)	*la presión arterial, presión de sangre*
blood test (n.)	*el examen de la sangre*
blood vessel (n.)	*la vena, el vaso sanguíneo*
blow (strike to body) (n.)	*el golpe*
blurred vision (n.)	*la vista nublada*

body (n.)	*el cuerpo*
boil, carbuncle (n.)	*el grano enterrado, carbunclo*
boil (v.)	*hervir*
bone (n.)	*el hueso*
bottle (n.)	
baby's	*la teta, pacha*
any other kind	*la botella*
bowel (n.)	*el intestino, la tripa*
bowel movement (n.)	*el excremento, la caca* °
bowel movement (v.)	*defecar, hacer caca* °
boy (n.)	*el muchacho*
brain(s) (n.)	*los sesos, el cerebro*
break (v.)	*quebrar, romper*
breast (n.)	*el pecho*
breast feed (v.)	*dar el pecho, mamar*
breathe (v.)	*respirar, resollar*
breathing (n.)	*la respiración, el resuello*
bring (v.)	*traer*
broken (adj.)	*quebrado, -a, roto, -a*
bronchitis (n.)	*la inflamación de los pulmones,*
	la bronquitis
bruise (n.)	*el moretón, morete*
bullet (n.)	*la bala*
bullet wound (n.)	*el balazo*
burn (n.)	*la quemada*
burn (v.)	*quemar*
burning sensation (n.)	*el ardor*
buttock (n.)	*la nalga*
callus (n.)	*el callo*
cancer (n.)	*el cáncer*
candy (n.)	*los dulces*
capsule (n.)	*la cápsula*
carrier (n.)	*el, la portador, -a, de enfermedad*
cast (n.)	*el calote, el yeso*
cataract (n.)	*la catarata*
catarrh (n.)	*el catarro*
catch a disease (v.)	*contraer una enfermedad*

°Note: May be considered vulgar outside the hospital situation, but is often better understood by children.

catheter (n.)	*el catéter, tubo*
cavity (dental) (n.)	*los caries, la cavidad dental, el diente podrido*
change of life (n.)	*el cambio de vida*
cheek (n.)	*la mejilla, el cachete*
cheese (n.)	*el queso*
chest (n.)	*el pecho*
chicken pox (n.)	*la viruela loca, varicela, viruela de gallina*
child (n.)	
boy	*el niño*
girl	*la niña*
childbirth (n.)	*el parto*
chill(s) (n.)	*el escalofrío, calosfrio*
chin (n.)	*la barba, barbilla*
choke (v.)	*ahogarse, atorarse*
chronic disease (n.)	*la enfermedad crónica*
clean (adj.)	*limpio, -a*
clinic (n.)	*la clínica*
close (v.)	*cerrar*
clot (blood) (v.)	*cuajar*
clot (n.)	*el cuajarón, el coágulo*
clothes (n.)	*la ropa*
cod liver oil (n.)	*el aceite de pescado*
cold (adj.)	*frío, -a*
cold (illness) (n.)	*el resfriado*
colic (n.)	*el cólico*
come (v.)	*venir*
come back (v.)	*volver*
comfortable (adj.)	*cómodo, -a, agusto, -a*
complain (v.)	*quejarse*
complication (n.)	*la complicación*
condom (n.)	*el hule, preservativo*
congestion (n.)	*la congestión*
congested (stuffed up) (adj.)	*constipado, -a*
constipated (adj.)	*estreñido, -a*
constipation (n.)	*el estreñimiento*
contact (n.)	*el contacto*
contagious (adj.)	*contagioso, -a*
continue (v.)	*seguir*
contraceptive (n.)	*el anticonceptivo*
convulsion (n.)	*el ataque, la convulsión*

cool (adj.)	*fresco, -a*
cotton (n.)	*el algodón*
cough (n.)	*la tos*
cough (v.)	*toser*
crab lice (n.)	*las ladillas*
cramp (n.)	
abdominal	*el retortijón, el torsón*
muscular	*el calambre*
crazy (adj.)	*loco, -a*
crippled (adj.)	*empedido, -a, lisiado, -a, cojo, -a*
cross-eyed (adj.)	*turnio, -a, bisojo, -a, bizco, -a*
croup (n.)	*la ronquera, crup*
crush (v.)	*machucar*
crutches (n.)	*las muletas*
cry (v.)	*llolor*
cut (n.)	*la cortada*
cut (v.)	*cortar*
cyst (n.)	*el quiste*
damage, harm (n.)	*el mal, daño*
dangerous (adj.)	*peligroso, -a*
dark (adj.)	*oscuro, -a*
dead (adj.)	*muerto, -a*
deaf (adj.)	*sordo, -a*
deafness (n.)	*la sordera*
death (n.)	*la muerte*
deep (adj.)	*profundo, -a*
defecate (v.)	*defecar, hacer caca* °
dehydrate (v.)	*deshidratar, perder fluidos del cuerpo*
deliver (give birth) (v.)	*tener niño, sanar de niño, dar a luz*
delivery (childbirth) (n.)	*el parto*
diabetes (n.)	*la diabetes, mucha azúcar en la sangre*
diaper (n.)	*el pañal*
diarrhea (n.)	*la diarrea*
die (v.)	*morir*
diet (n.)	*la dieta, el régimen*
difficulty (n.)	*la dificultad*
digestion (n.)	*la digestión*

°Note: May be considered vulgar outside the hospital situation, but is often better understood by children.

diptheria (n.)   *la difteria*
dirty (adj.)   *sucio, -a, puerco, -a*
disease of . . . (n.)   *la enfermedad de . . .*
disinfectant (n.)   *el desinfectante*
dislocated (adj.)   *dislocado*
dizziness (n.)   *el vértigo, las tarantas*
dizzy (adj.)   *vertiginoso, -a, atarantado, -a*
doctor (n.)   *el doctor, médico*
dose (n.)   *la medida*
double vision (n.)   *la vista doble*
douche (n.)   *el lavado vaginal*
drain (v.)   *vaciar*
drink (v.)   *beber, tomar*
drown (v.)   *ahogarse*
drugstore (n.)   *la botica, farmacia*
drug (n.)   *la droga*
drug addict (n.)   *el, la drogadicto, -a*
drug addiction (n.)   *la drogadicción, dependencia*
                                            farmacológica

drunk (adj.)   *borracho, -a*
dry (adj.)   *seco, -a*
dry (v.)   *secar*
dysentery (n.)   *la disentería (el cursio)*
dyspnea (n.)   *la dificultad al respirar*
dysuria (n.)   *dolor al orinar*

each (adj.)   *cada*
ear (n.)
   external   *la oreja*
   internal   *el oído*
earache (n.)   *el dolor de oído*
ear wax (n.)   *la cerilla, el cerumen*
eat (v.)   *comer*
eat breakfast (v.)   *desayunarse, almorzar°*
eczema (n.)   *la eczema, herpe*
eggs (n.)   *los huevos, blanquillos*
elbow (n.)   *el codo*
elevator (n.)   *el ascensor, elevador*
emergency (n.)   *la emergencia, el caso urgente*

°Note: *Almorzar* means to eat breakfast in New Mexico.

enema (n.)	*la lavativa, enema*
epidemic (n.)	*la epidemia*
epilepsy (n.)	*el ataque (de epilepsia)*
every (adj.)	*cada*
examination (n.)	*la examinación*
examine (v.)	*examinar*
exhaustion (n.)	*la fatiga*
eye (n.)	*el ojo*
eyelid (n.)	*el párpado*
face (n.)	*la cara*
faint (v.)	*desmayarse*
fat (adj.)	*gordo, -a*
fatigue (n.)	*la fatiga*
fear (n.)	*el miedo*
I am afraid.	*Yo tengo miedo.*
feces (n.)	*los feces, fecales, el excremento, la caca°, pase del cuerpo*
fee (n.)	*la cuenta*
feel (emotion, pain) (v.)	*sentir (se)*
feel (touch) (v.)	*tocar*
fester (v.)	*enconarse*
fetus (n.)	*el feto*
fever (n.)	*la fiebre, calentura*
finger (n.)	*el dedo*
fingernail (n.)	*la uña*
finish (v.)	*terminar*
flu (n.)	*la gripa, el catarro*
fly (insect) (n.)	*la mosca*
fontanel (n.)	*la mollera, fontanela*
foot (n.)	*el pie*
forehead (n.)	*la frente*
fracture (n.)	*la quebradura, fractura*
fracture (v.)	*quebrar (se), fractuar*
free (of charge) (adj.)	*gratis*
fresh (adj.)	*fresco, -a*
gain weight (v.)	*ganar peso, engordar*
gallbladder (n.)	*la vesícula biliar, hiel*

°Note: May be considered vulgar outside the hospital situation, but is often better understood by children.

gallstone (n.)	*la piedra de la hiel, el cálculo biliar*
gargle (v.)	*hacer gárgaras*
gas (n.)	*el gas*
germ (n.)	*el germen, microbio*
get sick (v.)	*enfermarse*
get up (v.)	*levantarse*
get well (v.)	*sanar*
girl (n.)	*la muchacha*
give (v.)	*dar*
glass (n.)	*el vaso*
glasses (eye-) (n.)	*los anteojos, las lentes, gafas*
goiter (n.)	*el bocio, buche, güegüecho*
good (adj.)	*bueno, -a*
gonorrhea (n.)	*la gonorrea*
gown (clinical) (n.)	*el camisón*
hair (n.)	*el pelo, cabello*
hand (n.)	*la mano*
hard (adj.)	*duro, -a*
have (v.)	*tener*
head (n.)	*la cabeza*
headache (n.)	*el dolor de cabeza*
heal (v.)	*sanar*
health (n.)	*la salud*
healthy person (n.)	*la persona sana, saludable*
hear (v.)	*oír*
heart (n.)	*el corazón*
heart attack (n.)	*el ataque del corazón*
heartburn (n.)	*las acedías, agruras*
heart trouble (n.)	*la enfermedad del corazón*
heat (n.)	*el calor*
heel (n.)	*el talón*
hematuria (n.)	*la sangre en el orín, hematuria*
hemorrhage (n.)	*el desangramiento, la hemorragia*
hemorrhoids (n.)	*los hemorroides, las almorranas*
hepatitis (n.)	*la hepatitis*
herb (n.)	*la yerba*
hernia (n.)	*la hernia*
high blood pressure (n.)	*la alta presión*
hip (n.)	*la cadera*
hives (n.)	*las ronchas*
hoarse (adj.)	*ronco, -a*

hospital (n.)	*el hospital*
hot (adj.)	*caliente*
hot flashes (n.)	*los calores, las llamaradas*
hunger (n.)	*el hambre*
I am hungry.	*Yo tengo hambre.*
hurt (v.)	*doler*
husband (n.)	*el esposo*
ill (adj.)	*enfermo, -a*
illness (n.)	*la enfermedad*
improve (v.)	*mejorar*
immunization (n.)	*la vacuna, inyección*
immunize (v.)	*vacunar*
inch (n.)	*la pulgada*
incision (n.)	*la cortada*
incubator (n.)	*la incubadora*
indigestion (n.)	*la indigestión, dispepsia*
infantile paralysis	*el polio, parálisis infantil*
infect (v.)	*infectar, contagiar*
fester	*enconarse*
infected (adj.)	*enconado, -a, infectado, -a*
infection (n.)	*la infección*
influenza (n.)	*la influenza, gripa*
ingrown toenail (n.)	*la uña enterrada, uña encarnada*
injection (n.)	*la vacuna, inyección*
injure (v.)	*lastimar, hacer daño*
injured (adj.)	*lastimado, -a*
injury (n.)	*la lastimadura, herida*
insane (adj.)	*demente, insano, -a*
inside (prep.)	*dentro de*
intestines (n.)	*los intestinos, las tripas†*
intoxicated (adj.)	*borracho, -a, intoxicado, -a*
isolate (v.)	*aislar, apartar*
itch (n.)	*el comezón*
jaw (n.)	*la quijada, mandíbula*
joint (n.)	*la coyuntura, articulación*
jaundice (n.)	*la piel amarilla, ictericia*
kidney (n.)	*el riñón*

†Southwestern localism

knee (n.)   *la rodilla*

laboratory test (n.)   *el análisis de laboratorio*
labor pains (n.)   *los dolores del parto*
laceration (n.)   *la cortada*
late (adj.)   *tarde*
  I'm late.   *Llego tarde.*
leave (v.)   *ir(se)*
left (adj.)   *izquierdo, -a*
leg (n.)   *la pierna*
let go of (v.)   *soltar*
lice (n.)   *los piojos*
lie down (v.)   *acostarse*
lift (v.)   *levantar*
light (n.)   *la luz*
limp (v.)   *cojear*
lip (n.)   *el labio*
liquid (n.)   *el líquido*
listen (to) (v.)   *escuchar*
liver (n.)   *el hígado*
look (at) (v.)   *mirar*
look (for) (v.)   *buscar*
loop (n.)   *el alambrito, lupo, la asa*
lose weight (v.)   *perder peso*
lukewarm (adj.)   *tibio, -a*
lump (n.)   *el hinchazón, la bola, el chinchón*
lung (n.)   *el pulmón*

make better (v.)   *aliviar*
make worse (v.)   *empeorar*
married (adj.)   *casado, -a*
massage (n.)   *la sobada, masage*
massage (v.)   *sobar, masagear*
measles (n.)   *el sarampión*
measure (v.)   *medir*
meat (n.)   *la carne*
medicine (n.)   *la medicina*
meningitis (n.)   *la meningitis*
menopause (n.)   *el cambio de vida, la menopausia*
menstrual period (n.)   *el tiempo del mes, la menstruación,*
                                            regla
mental hospital (n.)   *el hospital mental*

mental illness (n.)	*la enfermedad mental*
midwife (n.)	*la partera*
migraine (n.)	*la jaqueca, migraña*
milk (n.)	*la leche*
miscarriage (n.)	*el malparto; aborto involuntario*
mole (blemish) (n.)	*el lunar, la mancha*
mosquito (n.)	*el mosco, mosquito*
mouth (n.)	*la boca*
move (v.)	*mover(se)*
mucus (n.)	
nasal	*los mocos*
phlegm	*la flema*
mumps (n.)	*las paperas*
murmur, heart (n.)	*el soplo cardíaco, murmullo*
muscle (n.)	*el músculo, el muslo*
nail (metal) (n.)	*el clavo [clove]*†
nail (finger or toe) (n.)	*la uña*
name (n.)	*el nombre*
surname	*el apellido*
nap, to take a (v.)	*dormir en el día, tomar una siesta*
nausea (n.)	*el revuelto de estómago, basca, náusea*
navel (n.)	*el ombligo*
neck (n.)	
back of	*la nuca*
entire	*el cuello, pescuezo*
need (v.)	*necesitar*
needle, sewing (n.)	*la aguja de coser*
needle, syringe (n.)	*la aguja hipodérmica, jerginga*
nerve (n.)	*el nervio*
nervous (adj.)	*nervioso, -a*
nervousness (n.)	*la nerviosidad*
next (adj.)	*proximo, -a*
nipple (n.)	
breast	*el pezón*
bottle	*la teta, pancha, mamadera*
nose (n.)	*la nariz*
nosebleed (n.)	*salirle sangre de la nariz, la hemorragia nasal*

†Southwestern localism

nose drops (n.)	*las gotas nasales*
nostrils (n.)	*las narices, ventanas de la nariz*
nurse (v.)	*dar pecho, dar de mamar*
nurse (n.)	*la enfermera*

office (n.)	*la oficina*
often (adv.)	*á menudo, muchas veces*
oil (n.)	*el aceite*
ointment (n.)	*el ungüento, unto, la pomada*
open (v.)	*abrir*
operate (v.)	*operar*
operation (n.)	*la operación*
ounce (n.)	*la onza*
outside of (prep.)	*fuera de*
ovary (n.)	*el ovario*
oxygen (n.)	*el oxígeno*

pain (n.)	*el dolor*
palate (n.)	*el paladar*
palpitation (n.)	*la palpitación*
paralysis (n.)	*el parálisis*
patient (n.)	*el, la paciente*
penis (n.)	*el pene, miembro*
perspire (v.)	*sudar*
pharmacy (n.)	*la farmacia, botica*
phlegm (n.)	*la flema*
piles (n.)	*las almorranas*
pill (n.)	*la píldora, pastilla*
pillow (n.)	*la almohada*
pimple (n.)	*la espinilla*
place (v.)	*colocar, poner*
placenta (n.)	*la placenta*
play (v.)	*jugar*
pneumonia (n.)	*la pulmonía*
poison (n.)	*el veneno, la ponzoña*
polio (n.)	*el polio*
oral polio vaccine	*la vacuna oral contra el polio, las gotas de polio*
pound (n.)	*la libra*
pregnant (adj.)	*embarazada, en cinta, enferma de niño*
prenatal care (n.)	*el cuidado prenatal*

prescription (n.)	*la receta*
pull (v.)	*jalar*
pulse (n.)	*el pulso*
pupil (of eye) (n.)	*la niña del ojo, pupila*
pus (n.)	*la pus, materia*
push (v.)	*empujar*
put on (v.)	*ponerse*
quiet (v.)	*callar(se)*
quiet (n.)	*el silencio*
quiet (adj.)	*quieto, -a*
rabies (n.)	*la rabia*
raise (lift) (v.)	*levantar*
rash (n.)	
diffuse	*el sarpullido*
wheals, hives	*las ronchas*
recover (v.)	*sanar*
relapse (n.)	*la recaída*
relax (v.)	*relajarse, calmarse*
remove (v.)	*quitar*
resistance (n.)	*la resistencia*
respiration (n.)	*el resuello, la respiración*
rest (n.)	*el descanso*
rest (v.)	*descansar*
rheumatism (n.)	*el reumatismo, las reumas*
rib (n.)	*la costilla*
right (adj.)	*derecho, -a*
ringworm (n.)	*el empeine, la enfermedad de la piel*
room (n.)	*el cuarto*
rough (adj.)	*rasposo, -a, áspero, -a*
rubella fever (n.)	*la rubeola, sarampión de tres días*
rubdown (n.)	*la sobada*
rupture (n.)	*la ruptura, rotura*
rupture (burst) (v.)	*romper*
ruptured (adj.)	*roto, -a*
saliva (n.)	*la saliva, el esputo*
salve (n.)	*el ungüento, la pomada*
sample (n.)	*la muestra*
sanatorium (n.)	*el sanatorio*

scab (n.)	*la costra*
scale(s) (n.)	*la pesa, balanza*
scalp (n.)	*el casco, cuero cabelludo*
scar (n.)	*la cicatriz*
scarlet fever (n.)	*la fiebre escarlatina*
scissors (n.)	*las tijeras*
scorpion (n.)	*el alacrán*
scratch (n.)	*el rasguño, rascado*
scratch (v.)	
hurt	*rasguñar*
to relieve itch	*rascar(se)*
scrub (surgically) (v.)	*lavar, refregar, fregar*
see (v.)	*ver*
seizure (n.)	*el ataque, la convulsión*
serious (adj.)	*grave, serio, -a*
sexual relations (n.)	*las relaciones sexuales*
sharp pain (n.)	*el dolor agudo, clavado*
sheet (bed-) (n.)	*la sábana*
shiver (v.)	*temblar, tiritar*
shock (fright) (n.)	*el susto*
shot (injection) (n.)	*la inyección*
shoulder (n.)	*el hombro*
sick (adj.)	*enfermo, -a*
sickness (n.)	*la enfermedad*
side (n.)	*el lado*
sign (n.)	*la seña*
sinusitis (n.)	*la sinusitis*
sit down (v.)	*sentarse*
size (n.)	*el tamaño*
skin (n.)	*el cuero, la piel*
skull (n.)	*el cráneo [la calavera]†*
sleep (v.)	*dormir*
sleeve (n.)	*la manga*
sling (n.)	*la banda, el cabestrillo*
smallpox (n.)	*la viruela*
smell (v.)	*oler*
smell (n.)	*el olor*
smoke (v.)	*fumar*
smoke (n.)	*el humo*
snake (n.)	
nonpoisonous	*la serpiente, culebra no venenosa*
rattlesnake	*la víbora, culebra de cascabel*
sneeze (v.)	*destornudar*

soap (n.)	*el jabón*
soak (v.)	*remojar*
soft (adj.)	*blando, -a, suave*
sole (of foot) (n.)	*la planta del pie*
sore (n.)	*la llaga*
sore throat (n.)	*la garganta inflamada*
speak (v.)	*hablar*
specialist (n.)	*el especialista*
specimen (n.)	*la muestra, espécimen*
spell (v.)	*deletrear*
spider (n.)	*la araña*
black widow	*la viuda negra*
spinal tap	*horadación espinal, punción lumbar*
spine (n.)	*el espinazo, la columna vertebral*
spit (v.)	*escupir*
spit (n.)	*la saliva*
splint (v.)	*entabillar*
splinter (n.)	*la astilla*
spot (n.)	*la mancha*
sputum (n.)	*el esputo (de los pulmones)*
sprain (v.)	*torcer, desconcertar*
sprained (adj.)	*torcido, -a, desconcertado, -a*
spread (v.)	*destender*
squeeze (v.)	*apretar*
stand up (v.)	*parar(se), ponerse de pie*
stay (v.)	*quedarse*
steam (n.)	*el vapor*
stick out (v.)	*sacar*
stiff (adj.)	*tieso, -a*
sting (of an insect) (n.)	*el piquete, la punzada, picadura*
sting (v.)	*picar*
stitch (n.)	*la costura, puntada*
stomach (n.)	*el estómago [la panza]*†
stomach ache (n.)	*el dolor de estómago*
stone (n.)	*la piedra, el cálculo*
stool specimen (n.)	*la muestra de excremento, muestra de lieces fecales*
straight ahead (adv.)	*derecho*
straighten (v.)	*enderezar*
strength (n.)	*la fuerza*

†Southwestern localism

stroke (n.)   *el ataque cerebral, el accidente*
                                     cerebrovascular
strong (adj.)   *fuerte*
suddenly (adv.)   *de repente*
suffer (v.)   *sufrir*
sunburn (n.)   *la quemadura de sol*
suicide (n.)   *el suicidio*
suppository (n.)   *el supositorio, calillo*
surname (n.)   *el apellido*
swallow (v.)   *tragar*
sweat (n.)   *el sudor*
sweat (v.)   *sudar*
swell (v.)   *hinchar*
swollen (adj.)   *hinchado, -a*
symptom (n.)   *la síntoma*
syphilis (n.)   *la sífilis*
syringe (n.)   *la jeringa, aguja hipodérmica*

take (v.)   *tomar*
   Take this medicine.   *Tome esta medicina.*
take care of (v.)   *cuidar*
take off (v.)   *quitarse*
   Take off your undershirt.   *Quítese la camiseta.*
tape (n.)   *la tela, cinta*
tapeworm (n.)   *la lombriz (la lombriz solitaria)*
taste (to try) (v.)   *probar*
taste (v.)   *saber á, tener buen (mal) sabor,*
                                     saborear
   It doesn't taste bad.   *No sabe feo. No tiene mal sabor.*
tea (n.)   *el té*
tear (v.)   *romper*
tears (crying) (n.)   *las lágrimas*
teaspoonful (n.)   *la cucharadita*
temperature (n.)   *la temperatura*
tense (adj.)   *tenso, -a, nervioso, -a*
test (n.)   *el examen*
test (v.)   *examinar*
tetanus (n.)   *el tétano*
therapy (n.)   *el tratamiento*
thigh (n.)   *el muslo*
thirsty (to be) (v.)   *tener sed*

throat (n.)	*la garganta*
thumb (n.)	*el dedo gordo*
thyroid (n.)	*la tiroides*
tick (insect) (n.)	*la garrapata*
tinnitus (n.)	*el sumbido del oído, la tinitus*
tire (v.)	*cansar(se)*
tired (adj.)	*cansado, -a*
toe (n.)	*el dedo del pie*
toenail (n.)	*la uña del pie*
toenail (ingrown) (n.)	*la uña enterrada, uña encarnada*
toilet (n.)	*el excusado, baño, privado, comun*
tongue (n.)	*la lengua*
tonsilitis (n.)	*la tonsilitis*
tonsils (n.)	*las almígdalas*
too much, too many (adv., adj.)	*demasiado*
tooth (n.)	
incisor	*el diente incisivo*
molar	*la muela*
toothache (n.)	*el dolor de muela, dolor de diente*
tooth decay (n.)	*los dientes podridos, las caries dental*
touch (v.)	*tocar*
trachea (n.)	*la traquea, el gaznate*
tranquilizer (n.)	*la calmante, tranquilizante*
treatment (n.)	*el tratamiento*
tube (n.)	*el tubo*
tuberculin test (n.)	*la prueba por tuberculina*
tuberculosis (n.)	*la tisis, tuberculosis [tis]†*
tumor (n.)	*el tumor*
turn around (or over) (v.)	*voltearse*
twisted (adj.)	*torcido, -a*
typhoid fever (n.)	*la fiebre tifoidea*
ulcer (n.)	*la úlcera*
umbilicus (n.)	*el ombligo*
umbilical cord (n.)	*el cordón umbilical*
undernourished (adj.)	*desnutrido*
urethra (n.)	*la uretra*
urinalysis (n.)	*el análisis de los orines, análisis urinario*

†Southwestern localism

urinate (v.)	*orinar*
urine (n.)	*la orina, el orín*
uterus (n.)	*la matriz, el útero*
vaccinate (v.)	*vacunar*
vaccination (n.)	*la vacunación*
vagina (n.)	*la vagina*
vegetables (n.)	*la verdura, las legumbres*
vein (n.)	*la vena*
vision (n.)	*la vista*
vitamin (n.)	*la vitamina*
vomit (v.)	*vomitar*
waist (n.)	*la cintura*
wait (v.)	*esperar*
wake up (v.)	*despertar(se)*
walk (v.)	*andar, caminar*
warm, lukewarm (adj.)	*tibio, -a*
wart (n.)	*la verruga, el mezquino*
wash (v.)	
oneself	*lavarse*
watch (care for) (v.)	*cuidar*
water (n.)	*el agua*
wax (ear) (n.)	*la cerilla, el cerumen*
watery (adj.)	*blandito, -a, aguoso, -a*
weak (adj.)	*débil*
weakness (n.)	*la debilidad*
wean (v.)	*destetar*
week (n.)	*la semana*
weigh (v.)	*pesar*
weight (n.)	*el peso*
well (adj., adv.)	*bien*
wet the bed (v.)	*mojar la cama*
wheal (n.)	*la roncha*
wheeze (v.)	*respirar con dificultad*
whiskey (n.)	*el "whiskey"*
whooping cough (n.)	*la tos ferina*
wife (n.)	*la esposa, mujer*
wine (n.)	*el vino*
womb (n.)	*la matriz*
work (n.)	*el trabajo*
worm (n.)	*la lombriz, el gusano*

worry (n.)	*la preocupación, pena*
worry (v.)	*preocuparse [apenarse]*†
wound (n.)	*la herida*
wrist (n.)	*la muñeca*
x-ray (n.)	*la radiografía [retrato del x-ray]*†
x-ray (v.)	*radiografiar*

†Southwestern localism